Spit (verb) in my mouth

Kelsey Marie Harris

Spit (Verb) in My Mouth ©2020 by **Kelsey Marie Harris**. Published in the United States by Vegetarian Alcoholic Press. Not one part of this work may be reproduced without expressed written consent from the author. For more information, please contact vegalpress@gmail.com

For my three favorite Franks
Sinatra, Ocean, The Bunny

Contents

6. When I die, bury me a tree
7. Green Bay Road
8. Oh baby, I like it raw
9. Ode to social media
10. The lame buffalo is left behind
11. You think you want to keep your R Kelly albums but it's really just the Stockholm Syndrome
12. Hashtag roadkill
13. I dreamed of you dead again
14. Feet are just weird leg hands
15. Seasonal repression
26. Pink Frosting
17. What kind of bee gives milk?
18. The color blind cannot fly planes
19. Seasonal Depression
20. Spit (verb) in my mouth
21. Things you can't unhear
22. What that mouth do?
23. Self fertilization is a poor strategy for long term survival
24. Hallelujahed
25. Where is my activation kit?
26. Flagged
27. Inadequate
28. Aubade for creation, or God's wet dream
29. To the child who accidentally stumbles upon my poetry...
30. Skinny dipping with dick cheese
32. Coup De Grâce
33. Taint of race

34. Ass clapping for John Denver
35. Orgasm isn't enough
36. Ode to nursing
37. Ruminate
38. Aretha Franklin without a bra
39. Candid
40. 40 reasons my vagina itches
42. Awkward turtles
43. Word on the street
44. #getyourlife
45. Pinkest thoughts
46. Uptown Pub
47. Lucid
48. The revolution will not be televised
49. Deadbeat in spring
50. Glow-up
51. Irony
52. I don't shave my pussy, a defense
53. Hey service dog, don't bite off my cancer face
54. Palindrome Mandala
55. We'd Also watch Angel
56. Mammogram
57. Sex Wound
58. Rapture
59. Temporomandibular joint dysfunction
60. Requiem for a squirrel
61. Regurgitate
63. I'm a dirty, dirty bitch
65. Will and testament

...But at the end of the day,
none of my poems are "Frank Ocean" enough,
and therefore inadequate

When I die, bury me a tree

> There's a dead squirrel on the deck
> It's big and it's warm
> It's super dead, but its nerves haven't caught the hint
> The flies latched on immediately, almost shamefully
> And then I thought maybe they were collecting its soul

And then I thought maybe flies are angels

Green Bay Road

I drive with the radio off so I can hear what the world sounds like on my way home. The white noise of the road helps me notice things I'd otherwise miss for tunnel vision. If I walk on this road alone at night, I probably won't get raped. I might find a cool frog. I remember how much simpler the world seems from inside a car. How much quicker it would be to drive across a field than to walk. I look at the houses. I try to guess their property value. I try to guess who would shoot me for stepping on their property. How many doors are safe to knock on. When the speed limit slows to 35 I feel the pressure that occurs between work and home. I consider veering into the other lane. I look into the windows of houses. I admire their decor and their clutter. I hope to see someone naked, or making love. I watch the cars around me. I wonder if they are anxious like me. If they are distracted. If they are dependent on the radio.

Oh baby, I like it raw

    Your mother's lips are mirror images of your labia majora
The skin of your lips is identical to the skin of your asshole
    Spit on the tissue before wiping the asshole
Taylor Swift says don't wash your legs
    Or your chicken
Taylor Swift's legs are more seasoned than her chicken
    If you wouldn't soap your lips you shouldn't soap your asshole
Spit, then wipe, front to back
If you wouldn't rub shit on your mother's lips
You shouldn't rub it on your vagina
Rub your chicken on your mother's vagina

Ode to social media

When all else fails, cut off your thumbs

The lame buffalo is left behind

In the war on masculinity, the hyper masculine shall fight back with crossbows, brass knuckles, a horde of ligers, overcompensation, and tufted shields of chest hair. Butt plugs shall be distributed to ward off sodomy by the raging effeminate.

You think you want to keep your R Kelly albums but it's really just the Stockholm Syndrome

>Let's lay in bed with our demons
>be naked with them
>fall asleep with them
>breath their demon breath
>lay with them at daybreak suck
>in their morning breath
>pick their noses
>wipe it on our pillow
>play in their navals
>morning sex our demons awkward
>in sunlight so
>we can't hide our sex face
>cum in our demons
>play with it between
>our fingers
>let it dry on our skin
>invite them
>to stay for breakfast
>eat our heart
>the last of our cereal
>and leave our
>piss soaked bodies
>hollow on kitchen island

Hashtag roadkill

It's one of those nights if you were dying on the side of the road someone would likely find you. If you were dying on the side of the road, I'd find you and shame you for dying so publicly. Dying out in the open on a night like this as if nothing is sacred anymore. I die under the porch, or in the drawer, or under a rock the way death is intended. I die off the grid. You die on this busy road for prestige. How many likes will you get for dying this way? How viral will go your demise? How validated will you feel when your heart stops and everyone approves of its last beat? I'm looking down on you from my secret dying tree trolling you as if my death is more authentic. As if dead isn't dead.

I dreamed of you dead again

I've realized subconsciously I'm better at grief
but I wonder is good grief healthy or if you die would you rather I be
an emotional wreck for you and since you're dead is it as much a
matter of what you prefer as keeping up appearances
who should I keep them for
and how should I set my intention
the act of setting intention in itself feels like manipulation
but if it's not you I'm manipulating do I care
is my grief any less grief if it shows up as indifference

Feet are just weird leg hands

More often than not life is a hard dick and we are not consenting vaginas. Sometimes life is like a man you don't want to be left in a room alone with. Life will show you its ballsack when you're walking through the park. Life ejaculates in your soup and tea bags your coffee.

Seasonal repression

I crawled out from under my rock expecting warm weather. It's still raining. The more I'm around people the lonelier I realize I am. I'm meditating. An elephant's foot is pressed against my chest. To focus on breathing is labor. To focus on my heartbeat is terrifying. I'm almost sure I could burst it if I try. I'm afraid I will try. Some people relax by meditating, or masturbating, or painting. I did all three. I'm still anxious. Now I have shame face. I can't face my children. They know I'm incapable of love, but they commend my efforts. Who taught them empathy? How do they know tolerance when their mother is a pet rock with a painted face? A kindness rock. Nice quotes on small cold slabs. Perpetually meaningless in all ways except intention, the most worthless noun.

Pink Frosting

We probably shouldn't talk about the fog
Or how Kwik Trip coffee makes me shit like I'm dying
I don't want to talk about wet boxes
But mildew tastes like pink frosting
No matter how many cough drops you suck
I shouldn't read the boxes
They tell me "don't cut with blades"
It feels condescending
It feels invasive
I feel vulnerable
The tape never sticks
The tape gun is cheap
I don't want to tell you I'm flaky
So, I'm a tape gun

What kind of bee gives milk?

This is a breast in the shape of a poem

It is not perfect

It may grow cancer one day

For now, appreciate it for its mild suppleness and moderate elasticity

The color blind cannot fly planes

Fetused between the floorboards, the soft stench of abortion you can't scrub out. Possess not, scowl at possession. Sell your kidneys. Sell your pussy. Sell your soul. People are like clouds. They follow you around and piss on you when they're angry. We are fuck trophies, textured like crotch rot, our only difference the direction of the grain. Some of us are thorned and wilted parts, some of us soft petals. We all die and shit after.

Seasonal Depression

The Sun is like your first love
Days the sun doesn't shine are like when your first love forgets to call
Because they are out fucking somebody else
Like California
The Sun is always fucking California

Spit (verb) in my mouth

I don't know how to be a person, but I try really hard every day. I can't tell if I have empathy, or if I've learned how to mimic feeling. I'm not sure if I have memories, or if I'm using context clues. Sometimes I cry because I want to and can't. Sometimes I think God made me in a manic state. Sometimes I think when God made me, they were late for something.

Things you can't unhear

The song "On Top of Spaghetti" is a metaphor for losing your virginity.

What that mouth do?

People believe in me like Jesus.
Which is to say, they don't .
You follow me to the end of the flat earth and fall off.
I keep going, because it's round.
I fall and scrape my knee, it's bleeding.
It's trending blood.
This is America, Ferrera.
Low key, we'd all fuck Ugly Betty.
I'm your beautiful daddy.
The world's my deadbeat child.
I'm preaching to the choir, no one is listening.
They are busy singing,
at my face.
It's aggressive.
I talk by not talking.
I crip walk on water.
I smile, bitch.
I beat life, and now I'm sleepy.

Self-fertilization is a poor strategy for long term survival

I bicycle past your dilapidated house. You are sad, but I am happy because I am biking. The bright ribbons on my basket make me feel so alpha. My hot tongue melts a hole in the center of my Cookies n' Cream ice cream. I push it in and out. I pretend I'm Dalmatian sex.

Hallelujahed

I ordered the Holy Spirit
but all they had was Sierra Mist

Where is my activation kit?

If you give a man a fish he will eat for a day
If you teach a man to fish,
he will probably still use DoorDash.

Flagged

I'm old now and unsure if summer comes and goes quicker or if I'm more impatient. The days are short but the weeks are too long. Lately I've remembered my dreams and in them everyone is dying. Google says it's because my relationships will change. I say Google is naive to assume I don't simply want to kill everyone. Ironically, I'm naive to assume that isn't precisely what she means.

Inadequate

The heat of my crotch was not sufficient enough to warm my snack cake by the time I got to work, and I'm insecure about that. I sat on that thing for a good 20 minutes, and it's still cold at the center, like my heart. Four ibuprofen and a missort. The patriarchy is slacking off again. Go tilt yourself and put your ass into it. A down stack is as good as a hiit workout. Hold the invisible quarter between your butt cheeks. Hold it there your entire break. Hold it during pre-depart. Don't drop ass in the fluid trailer.

Aubade for creation, or God's wet dream

Morning broke its skin
Retreated
down the sky
Its dead roots uncurled
And sap swelled
Even in the sun
Looped over
Sour breath
On stiff knees
A cock
Exploded in purple
And gold
Sunlight broke open
And passion covered us
all

To the child who accidentally stumbles upon my poetry...

Don't show your mother.
Hide them in that spot under your mattress reserved for porn and love letters.
The filthiest acts I've described have been done by your parents.
It's probably how you were conceived.
You probably were an accident.
Sometimes in life you have to say penis a lot.
It's okay to write a sexy poem about Jesus.
They will try to convince you there are no voices.
Listen to the voices.

Skinny dipping with dick cheese

My booty ate the sun dress
I tried to free the sun dress
My booty ate my arm

I snort the ashes of my dead goldfish
I wake up in a third dimension
Trapped inside a glass bowl

I grind against the crotch buckle
I orgasm into the other lane
The cherry atop a 12 car pile up

I hide the cheese in my underwear
I discover it the next day
The crumbs make an excellent salad topper

I draw pictures of you naked
I hide them in obvious places
You find them and cry a little

I hide loogies in your couch
I smear them between the crevices
You find them instead of the remote

I pass one bloody egg in the bathtub
I chase it with my thumb
It wriggles away like a neurotic guppy

I masturbate to your diary

I cum on the tear stained pages

Your sad thoughts excite me sexually.

Coup de Grâce

There will be no gingers post apocalypse

I cream corn while I turn in my grave

No one will lend me a cup of sugar

Or a bowl of empathy

Being born with no soul does not render sympathy

Life is a sombrero

Life is a jury

A jury is a sombrero

Taint of race

There were bloodstains on the mattress. He told me not to worry, they were more menstruation than murder. The room was heavy. Acid filled scrotum chandeliered from the ceiling like livestock in a meat locker. The walls mumbled an unfamiliar blues riff. I could hardly make out the lyrics "...I am Charlie Sheen, I am Sara Baartman, I am your pseudo sex symbol, I look good in leather..." The sun peeked through the wood paneling, a voyeur straining to catch a glimpse of Nudie Judy, fondling the busted glass on the floor. Needless to say, it was a ballsy set up. I asked Jesus what he put in my drink. He said he slipped me a Holy Roofy. He removed his Rhinestone Cowboy belt buckle. Its clink on the nightstand echoed, and I watched the sound waves vibrate off the metal like psychedelic heat waves. Suddenly the hills were alive with the sound of his zipper and they were shouting, "Get the fuck out you stupid cunt!" I opened my mouth to scream but all that came out was a squirrel monkey. It flipped me off before scurrying beneath the door. The mundane had been set ablaze. The walls became a thousand weeping eyes. An anaconda unfolded itself from his pants. Jesus pulled a flute from his back pocket and proceeded to charm his snake penis. At full mass it unhinged its jaw and swallowed me whole. I woke up in an alley, nude and covered in feathers. There was a strange sensation in my mid-section. I peeled open my vagina and pulled out a note. "Congratulations, you have been immaculately conceptioned."

Ass clapping for John Denver

We thick   tongue
       We eater of   children
We   shallow dish fat
       We golden   palms
We paliform   spangle
We warping hand   shaped   palmiped palter
       We moist   in all parts
We nipple shaped   projection
       We pappus mock moon
We sorry
We parasite   vomit
       We titmouse
        We young   salmon
We paint   thick
We pussy   pop
       We Christian of chin
We hang horse   by the legs
       We imaginary solution
We shaped like a   kneecap
        We coxswain
       We pavonine
We full of   cows
       We pedicle
We pettitoes
We   poppy red

Orgasm isn't enough

You won't be content until your heart explodes. Euphoria is only experienced in death. Death is complete. You can't chase the high.

Ode to nursing

You anti-psychotic tongue thrusting into a blood-borne peri-meatus.
You infected stoma.
You busted sack of intestinal drainage soaking into a piss-stained curity.
You dementiaed resident voiding in your roommate's blooming foxglove.
You festered, pussed pressure ulcer.
You diarrhea flowing from an incontinent bowel.
You abusive, burned-out third-shifter.
You attempt at applying condom catheters to flaccid, geriatric penises.
You exposed, pendulic scrotum.
You angel of mortem lurking behind privacy curtains.
You mucusy death rattle.
You mottled nail beds.
You Cheyne-Stokes.
You body propped, posed and rigor-mortised.
You military time of death.

Ruminate

As a child, instead of poems, I'd write body parts.
I'd stash them in every room.
If you found yourself nervous in the kitchen,
you'd only have to reach around the cereal,
to make everyone in the room naked.

If I fall in the woods and no one is there to hear me scream
it is still awkward, and a slight overreaction.
The sensation in my arm makes me wonder if I had a heroin addiction
in a past life, or as a child.
My former addiction is a repressed memory.
As a child, I always knew I'd get vagina cancer.

Aretha Franklin without a bra

This is a middle finger in the shape of a poem

Candid

There are days a wad of 2 ply must stand in for a tampon. We can't always live up to our full potential. Teach your daughters, there are times we must scratch the crust off our panties and ride them out another day. Douching does not rid today of its sorrow. Only tomorrow of its strength.

40 reasons my vagina itches

Dawn dish detergent bubble bath
Influenza
Cancer
The summer sausage experiment
The illuminati
Climate change
Wearing panties
Not wearing panties
Secondhand panties
Secondhand couch
Public toilets
Antidepressants
Seasonal depression
Dairy
Gentrification
Shaving
Not shaving
Birth control
Pesticides
Botflies
Chip crumbs
Mercury
Sulfate
Fluoride
Gluten
OCD
MSG

GMO

BPA

YMCA

I haven't peed today

The bees are dying

Lead paint

Morning traffic

Skipping breakfast

Improper hand washing

I wore these pants yesterday

I pulled the short straw

I missed a memo

You forgot to sneeze in your elbow

Awkward turtles

Jesus fish is farm raised and filled with mercury.
Limit consumption, or have weird babies.

Word on the street

I may have peed in your electric outlet
fortunately, it hasn't worked since the last time I peed in it

#getyourlife

Priorities and puzzle pieces are the same
In order, they create the bigger picture
In disarray, that fish may never have an eye
An eye for an eye leaves every horse blind
Necessary, maybe
For crossing burning bridges

Pinkest thoughts

I use my vagina as a bath toy. Not in a sexual nature. Like a child, playing with a bath toy. I open myself up and Kegel the water in. I hold it, then shoot it out. I imagine all the tiny bacteria being set free and the adventures ahead of them. I am entertained, only momentarily. I suddenly feel empty, as if I've lost friends.

I watch the yellow dissipate into the bath water. After the color fades, you don't realize you're soaking in your own piss. Secretly, among our pinkest thoughts, we are content with soaking in a personal pool of urine. The idea of sitting in someone else's is always off-putting.

Uptown Pub

When God has an orgasm
A poet gets a brand-new thought
And a baby angel gets its wings
With extra blue cheese

Lucid

I finally discovered the end of the rainbow. I fastened it around my neck and coaxed the leprechaun into my chocolate starfish. The perfect storm of anal rampage and auto asphyxiation, I masturbated with such rapid force, my skin rubbed off in my hands. This new element of pain sent my pleasure sensors into hyper drive. I ventured into a realm incomprehensible to mortals. My eyeballs froze and shattered like ice. Blood spat from my ears. I reached an orgasm so massive I spontaneously combusted. Pink mist and ejaculate coated the clouds. And that's how I was reincarnated as a unicorn.

The revolution will not be televised

Sometimes I turn on my GPS and deliberately go the wrong way

Deadbeat in spring

Mother earth is giving birth around our feet
You litter your responsibilities
And blow smoke in her face
Futures can't grow in radioactive soil
War is raging

War has taken all your glow sticks
Grab me by my biological property and
Call me Ivanka, Tiffany
Call me global warming
Finger fuck me and watch it flood in
Shreveport

Glow-up

The square longed to be a sexier polygon

Nonagon, maybe

Irony

Upon discovering two grey hairs on my vagina,
                I realized I'm still quite flexible for my age.

I don't shave my pussy, a defense

No city ordinance can citation the height of my woman weeds. My pubes are a protest of a thousand mighty women, locking arms in solidarity. You want to scale my fence. Enter unannounced. Jump around like a metalhead in a mosh pit. No sir. My cervical sanctuary is no mosh pit. It is a Mexican bakery filled with sweet Dulce de Leche. You will not bake your bread here. You will not crack my eggs or pour your sour man milk inside of me. My pubes are a barbed wire fence cultivated to macerate your flesh.

Hey service dog, don't bite off my cancer face

I spent the morning thinking about
mastectomy tattoos and eating
dirty chicken nuggets off the floor
of my car. I ate them fast, like an
animal, on account of not wanting
to share them with my toddler at
home. And my car is disgusting.
My filthy car is on the list of things
I vehemently blame on my
children. Everyone knows it would
still smell weird without them.

Palindrome Mandala

The leaf is dead

It is the jaded wind

Such is fuckery

In the leaf

Some see whimsy

Falling

And free

Crisp

Shades

Of red and brown

Gradient hues

Of red and brown

Shades

Crisp

And free

Falling

Some see whimsy

In the leaf

Such is fuckery

It is the jaded wind

The leaf is dead

We'd also watch Angel

All I know is I was 10. I blinked.
Now I'm 30. Sometimes I feel
like that Buffy episode where
she suddenly had a sister and
they didn't explain it.

Mammogram

My mother died on a frigid day in
November in a house with no furniture outside
of a hospital bed, a speaker box, and an independent
dinner table chair. She left behind a pair of reading
glasses, a box of water-damaged
photos, and the purple dress she died
in. I asked if she'd like to listen to music, what
song she'd like to hear. She looked at me, eyes full
of resentment, "Give me one reason to stay here."
God, I wish I had one.

Sex wound

I wipe my nose with my hand and find I've cut my palm open with my nose ring. Blood and snot mingle, pool down my lifeline. Retreat into the crevice of my wrist. It stings and glistens like a sex wound.

Rapture

My face is full of flesh wounds. Anxiety
dictates I excavate my adult acne. Every
morning I pull into my driveway
and pick at my face with my filthy
work hands. I can almost hear
the bumps scream bloody
murder each time I
macerate them
with my dirty
fingernails.
I know
this is
redundant
but it's as
if my
bumps
are alive
and even
uninvited
they
have
souls
and I
have
a God complex.

Temporomandibular joint dysfunction

I bite off the heads of my coworkers

Gnaw them between my crossbite

Crack their skulls in my clenched jaw

For not knowing how to count

I spit their chewed heads on dolly

Scoot them lane to lane

Wild, reckless, abandoned

I only speak in barks and bitches and move the fuck out of my ways

I almost don't remember I'm a Pisces anymore

I almost don't remember this used to be fun

In the winter the neon coveralls and stolen dock hats

When Stephanie was here and we'd

Nickname the truck drivers

Back when slacking off and cartwheels

Twerking in frozen fluid trailers

Now I push these pallet jacks alone

In quiet coffee fueled rage

My coworkers, headless

tip toeing behind me

Trying their best not to step on the

eggshells I leave in my path

Requiem for a squirrel

A squirrel stood over another
Flattened on the road

Could have been a lover,
stranger, or nemesis

All, I think, inflict the same
Burden of empathy

Variant degrees on a
moment of longing

Despite my best effort to
swerve, the squirrel

almost certainly, dove underneath my car
the sound of the skull

Crack beneath my tire
Too loud for its size

A dirge of sorts

Regurgitate

Indifferent to sunrise,
I'm an aubade. Life
is a run on joke, God,
a washed up comedian.
I'm all punchline,
mocking life like a
plastic shrub.
I'm questioning my need
for sustenance. I don't
believe in forgiveness
or you or saying
you're welcome.
I don't know luck or
its contrast. All I know
is none of my
thoughts are my
thoughts and social media
solidifies it so.

All I know is you
are trash, subconsciously
dictating all
of my decisions.
You in your fall colors,
frizzy braids, autonomy.
All I feel are dead
leaves. I want
subtle underarm hair.
I want to be messy
with intention.
I want my mental illness
glorified. I want it a foundation
for friendships to grow.
Toxic ones, that
fuel poems/ cut in the creases/
give me something
to post about.

I'm a dirty, dirty bitch

You can taste my plaque spit
and poo from my shit eating grin I got
pit stains and crotch crust on the
pants cus we dont wear

panties on this side of the grass
and we don't cut our grass and we
cum secretly to ourself all day and
wear it on our pussy lips we let it

dry there only because there's
pleasure in the pain of ripping it
apart sort of like picking in your
nose and catching that good

booger the one wrapped around
your nose ring that drags along a
tail of snot but we're too grown to
eat it so we rub it between our

fingers till it crumbles and
disappears in the crack of the
couch to be with the rest of
whatever we've smeared down

there and we don't clean our
couch and we don't clean our

house and only think about
showers when it starts to itch then

wait an extra day cus dirty bitches
got endurance.

Will and testament

When I die, plaster my likeness on t-shirts and wristbands. Selfie with my casket. Sign my body like your high school yearbook. Brand my initials on your first born. Worship me like God, or Oprah. Sell my dirty panties as keepsakes. Cut off my fingers and string them around your neck. Call out my name when you make love. Photoshop my face over pictures of your grandparents. Use me to rear your children. Stuff me with potpourri and display me on holidays. Prop me in your garden to scare away your crows. Modge-podge my skin over dresser drawers and coffee mugs. Add clever quotes like, "If you were me, you'd be here by now."

Thank you to my husband, Stephen. You were there while most of these poems were happening, and that couldn't have been easy. Thank you to my kids: Amore, Harlem, and Shakur. If I fail you completely, at least you'll have something to write about. Thank you Linda and James for loving me, and loving each other. Thank you Nicks: Demske, Ramsey, Ravnikar. Thank you Angela. Thank you Jen and Jenny. Thank you Kris and Clina. Thank you Alex. Thank you El Kid. Thank you Chad. Thank you Grimbol. Thank you Aaron. Thank you Russel Jaffey and *TLDR*. Thanks Amazon for being shitty, but inspiring. Thank you to all the presses and people that saw the method to my madness. Thank you Kelsey Hoff for helping me self-publish my first chapbook, *Fondled and Mangoed*. My chapbook *The Jolly Queef* was published by Vegetarian Alcoholic Press, thank you Freddy.

"Ode to Nursing" was published in *Verse Wisconsin*.

"40 Reasons my Vagina Itches" and an earlier version of "Deadbeat in Spring" were published in *The Rust Mil*. An earlier version of "Lucid" and "Taint of Race" were published by *Horror Sleaze Trash*. "What kind of bee gives milk" and "Aretha Franklin without a Bra" were published by *Forklift Ohio*.

www.ingramcontent.com/pod-product-compliance
Lightning Source LLC
Chambersburg PA
CBHW030137100526
44592CB00011B/927